To:

From:

S0-COO-691

MICROWAVE
solves fast meal problems

ISBN 1-56383-011-6

TABLE OF CONTENTS

Creating wonderful culinary cuisine with your microwave can be an exciting experience. The microwave is an excellent tool, when used properly, to compliment your cooking skills. Microwave cooking combined with the food processor, oven, stove and toaster-oven can make you responsible for rave reviews from your family and guests. One need not spend hours in the kitchen to produce lovely meals - just let everyone think you spent the time laboring over the feast. Enjoy your microwave, use your microwave, and learn to say thank you when the compliments come your way.

Zap It and Enjoy!

Rules of Thumb for the Microwave

1. Recipes in this book are based on microwaves with 600 to 650 watts.
2. Microwave cooking will vary depending on:
   a. Quantity of food. The more food, the more time because the same amount of "microwaves" are distributed at a time. Therefore 2 potatoes will take longer than 1 potato.
   b. Shape of food. thinner foods take less time than thicker foods. Try to place foods in the donut shape whenever possible. Food cooked in the microwave cooks from the outside to the inside.
   c. Starting temperature of food. Refrigerated foods take longer.
   d. Composition of recipes. "Microwaves" are attracted to sugar and fat. Foods with a high content of these ingredients will microwave faster.
3. Always use the shortest cooking times suggested. You can always add on more time but you can never subtract time.
4. If a recipe calls for stirring, it is important that this be done for even quality cooking.

5. Remember the final process in microwave cooking is the rest period.
6. To convert your favorite recipe for the microwave, try and find a comparable recipe in a microwave cookbook (basic quantity of ingredients) and use that recipe's timings.
7. Rule of thumb is that microwave cooking is ¼ that of conventional.
8. Reheat foods at 70% for best quality.
9. When defrosting foods, allow the same amount of resting time before you begin to cook the food (defrost 5 minutes, rest 5 minutes).
10. Remember to keep a glass of water in your microwave when it is not in use so there is not chance your machine will be run empty.
11. Dried on spill-over may be easily cleaned by microwaving 1 cup of water 2 minutes. Simply wipe up with a damp cloth. Your microwave should be wiped out with a damp cloth after each use. If there is condensation, use a paper towel to wipe away moisture.

12. Instruct all who will be using the microwave the basic procedures - no foil trays, not metal ties, proper power settings, piercing of certain foods, correct coverings and proper cooking times.

13. Test your utensils to be sure they are microwave-safe. Place 1 cup of water in the microwave next to the dish to be tested. Microwave on high 90 seconds. The water should be hot. If the dish is hot it is not microwave-safe.

14. Utensils for the microwave are glass, plastic, paper and wooden spoons. There are many microwave products on the market, select only what you need. Your basic needs should include 1-,2-,4- and 8-cup measuring cups, a slotted bacon rack, wooden spoons, 6 and 12 cup ring molds, muffin pan, custard cups, glass pie plates and 1-, 2-, 3- and 4-quart casserole dishes with lids.

15. When using a probe:
    a. Storage is in a drawer, NOT in the microwave.
    b. They are NOT dishwasher safe.
    c. They may NOT be used in an oven.

16.   A browning dish is not necessary, but if you do use one:
    a. Do not preheat for more than 7 minutes.
    b. Do not cover with wax paper or paper towels or plastic wrap.
    c. Remember to Always use a hot pad. The element will burn your fingers.
    d. The browning dish is the only thing you run your microwave on empty.
    e. Be careful where you place it when cooking is completed - it gets HOT and will burn the surfaces.
17. Use proper coverings to obtain proper moisture required for your recipe. For steamed effect vegetables - shellfish), use plastic wrap, making sure to vent one corner. For meats and casseroles, use wax paper. For bacon or sausage, use paper towels, this prevents splattering.
18. Foil may be used to shield certain foods. Recipes requiring foil are mentioned in the recipe. Only use foil when it is called for.
19. When using paper towels and paper plates, check to be sure they are NOT made from recycled products.
20. Salt draws moisture out of food cooked in the microwave. Salt after the food is cooked. Use garlic or onion powder instead of garlic or onion salt.

21. Snack foods such as crackers, pretzels, potato chips, popcorn and corn chips may be refreshened by arranging them on a paper plate. Microwave on high for 30 to 60 seconds and let rest 1 to 2 minutes.

22. Stale brown sugar need not be tossed. Place an apple wedge or a slice of bread inside the box. Microwave on high 45 to 60 seconds.

23. To soften 8 ounces of cream cheese, microwave at 30% for 50 to 60 seconds. Chocolate squares can be melted in their wrapper, no extra dish to clean. For 1 ounce, microwave on high 1 to 2 minutes.

24. When making yeast bread, use your temperature probe to heat the water to 115° F. for a perfect combination of the yeast and water.

25. When using recipes with a large sugar content (jellies, jam, candy) use an extra large container (8- or 12-cup).

26. Noodles and rice may be cooked in the microwave, but you will obtain a better quality if you use your stove.

27. When reheating yeast bread products, wrap them in a paper towel to retain moisture. This will prevent the bread from turning to rock.

28. To separate cold bacon slices with ease, microwave on high 15 to 20 seconds.
29. Rule of thumb for bacon, microwave on high 1 to 1½ minutes per slice.
30. To warm baby bottles or food, loosen caps and remove metal lids, microwave on high 20 to 30 seconds or until warm.
31. Parsley and other herbs dry beautifully in the microwave, no more waste. Place about 1 cup on a paper towel and microwave on high, 2 to 4 minutes. Crumble in paper towel.
32. Melt 16 ounces of caramels with 2 tablespoons water, microwave at 70% for 2 to 3 minutes. Stir every minute. Great for taffy apple or caramel sauce.
33. Egg whites may be brought to room temperature quickly. Microwave at 30% for 10 seconds per egg.
34. Citrus fruit will obtain more juice if microwaved. Lemons and oranges, microwave for 15 seconds; grapefruit, 30 seconds. Both on high.
35. Syrup for pancakes is wonderful warm. Remove cover and microwave at 50% for 30 seconds.

36. Saute mushrooms, onions and celery with unsalted butter. Place vegetables and butter in dish, microwave on high 1 to 2 minutes.

37. Clarifying butter is a breeze in your microwave. For ¼ cup (1 stick), place butter in measuring cup and microwave on high 40 seconds, then microwave at 50% for 1½ to 2 minutes. Skim off top layer.

38. To toast almonds or other nuts, place in a glass dish and microwave on high until brown, stirring every 60 seconds.

39. To defrost whipped toppings, microwave at 30%, 4¼ ounces for 30 seconds, 9 ounces for 60 seconds.

40. Brandy may be heated (great for flaming desserts), place 2 to 4 ounces in microwave-safe glass and microwave on high for 20 to 30 seconds.

41. Microwave a damp towel for a wonderful heat compress. Microwave on high for 1 to 2 minutes.

BREAKFAST & BRUNCH

EGGS - HINTS

Eggs must be handled with care because of their delicate make up. If not
properly prepared, they can explode, leaving a terrible mess to clean. Basic
rules to follow when microwaving eggs, are:

1. Do not cook eggs in their shells.
2. Use 50% or 70% when cooking poached or fried eggs.
3. Pierce the yolk and whites of poached or fried eggs with a
   toothpick. This will allow steam to escape so that they will
   not explode.

POACHED EGG

Place 1 egg in a custard cup. Pierce yolk and white with a toothpick. Cover
with wax paper. Microwave on medium, 50%, 45 to 60 seconds. Enjoy a
calorie-free egg.

HARD-BOILED EGGS

Place 2 eggs in a custard cup. Pierce yolks and whites. Cover with wax paper. Microwave at 70% for 50 to 60 seconds per egg. Rest 3 to 4 minutes. Wonderful for egg salad and potato salad.

SCRAMBLED EGGS

Place 2 eggs in a glass measuring cup. Whip eggs until well blended. Cover with wax paper. Microwave on high 1 minute. Stir. Microwave on high 30 to 60 seconds. Rest 1 minute. Cheese may be added during the "rest" period for cheese-scrambled eggs.

4 eggs: Microwave on high for 2½ to 3 minutes, stirring 2 times.
6 egg: Microwave on high for 3½ to 4½ minutes, stirring 2 times.

PIZZA EGGS

4 eggs
2 T. milk
1½ T. unsalted butter
Bacon, cooked and
  chopped

Onions
Green peppers
Tomato slices (thin)

Microwave butter in a 9 or 10" glass pie dish for 20 seconds. Whip eggs and milk until well blended. Add to melted butter. Cover with wax paper. Microwave on high 2 minutes. Add bacon, onions, green peppers and tomato. Microwave at 70% for 4 to 5 minutes. Rest 3 to 4 minutes.

SUNDAY MORNING DELIGHT

8 eggs
2 C. sharp Cheddar cheese,
  shredded
1 C. chopped onion

1 C. half and half
1 C. whipping cream
8 slices crustless day-old
  bread
2-quart buttered casserole

Blend eggs, half and half and cream until well blended. Add cheese and onions. Place 4 slices of bread in 2-quart buttered casserole dish. Add half of the egg mixture. Repeat. Refrigerate overnight. Microwave at 70% for 20 minutes. Rest 5 minutes. Serves 6 to 8.

BEAUTIFUL BRUNCH EGGS

8 slices crustless bread,
  cubed
3 C. Monterey Jack cheese,
  shredded
½ lb. sausage, cooked
  and well drained
6 eggs

1½ C. milk
1 C. half and half
1½ tsp. dry mustard
2 C. mushrooms, sauteed
1 can cream of mushroom
  soup, blended with ½ C
  milk

Combine eggs, milk, half and half and mustard. Blend well. Set aside. Place a layer of bread, then cheese and sausage in casserole. Pour egg mixture over sausage. Refrigerate overnight. Arrange mushrooms on top of casserole. Pour soup over casserole. Microwave on high 2 minutes. Microwave at 70% for 18 to 20 minutes. Rest 5 minutes.

HARD-BOILED EGG CASSEROLE

12 to 14 slices crisp bacon,
   crumbled

16 sliced hard-boiled eggs,
   cooked on stove
1 C. bread crumbs

CHEESE SAUCE:
4 T. unsalted butter
3 T. flour

1½ C. half and half
1 C. sharp Cheddar cheese,
   shredded

TO MAKE CHEESE SAUCE: Microwave butter in 2-cup measuring cup for 30 seconds on high. Blend in flour. Slowly add cream and blend well. Microwave on high for 1 minute, stir. Microwave on high for 1 minute, stir. Add cheese and blend.

Coat buttered casserole with 2 tablespoons bread crumbs. Place sliced eggs neatly in 2-quart buttered casserole. Add bacon. Pour cheese sauce over eggs. Sprinkle remaining bread crumbs over mixture. Microwave at 70% for 8 to 10 minutes. Rest 5 minutes.

CEREAL

Hot cereal made in the microwave has a tendency to boil over, be sure to use a proper dish to avoid extra clean up. Stirring is an important step in cooking cereal, for it prevents lumps from forming.

QUICK-COOKING OATMEAL

ONE SERVING: ¾ cup water and ⅓ cup cereal, microwave on high for 2½ minutes.
TWO SERVINGS: 1½ cups water and ⅔ cup cereal, microwave on high for 3½ minutes.
FOUR SERVINGS: 3 cups water and 1⅓ cups cereal, microwave on high for 6 minutes.

CREAM OF WHEAT

Combine cereal and water, stir 2 times.

ONE SERVING: ¾ cup water and 3 tablespoons cereal, microwave on high 2⅓ minutes.

TWO SERVINGS: 1½ cups water and 6 tablespoons cereal, microwave on high 3½ minutes.

FOUR SERVINGS: 2¾ cups water and ⅔ cup cereal, microwave on high 6 minutes.

UPSIDE-DOWN COFFEECAKE

TOPPING: Combine and set aside.
¼ C. brown sugar   *1 tsp. cinnamon*
½ C. nuts, chopped

CAKE: Combine all ingredients.
¼ C. flour   *1 tsp. cinnamon*
½ C. brown sugar   *½ tsp. cloves*
½ tsp. baking soda   *½ C. sour milk*
½ tsp. baking powder   *⅓ C. Crisco*
¼ tsp. salt   *1 egg*

Butter a 9" cake pan and line with wax paper, butter the wax paper. Press topping in bottom of pan. Pour cake batter over topping. Microwave on high for 5 to 6 minutes. Rest 5 minutes. Invert on serving plate. Drizzle with glaze. GLAZE: Combine ½ cup powdered sugar and 1 tablespoon milk.

REFRIGERATOR ROLL COFFEECAKE

5 T. brown sugar
3 T. unsalted butter
1 T. water

½ to ¾ C. chopped nuts
1-8 oz. refrigerator rolls

Place brown sugar, butter and water in a 6-cup ring mold. Microwave on high 1 minute. Stir. Place biscuits around mold. Microwave at 50% for 4 to 6 minutes. Rest 3 to 4 minutes. Invert on serving plate. The biscuits will appear pale to say the least. But this is an "upside-down" recipe. With all the glaze no one will notice. These should be eaten right after cooking because they dry out quickly.

ZUCCHINI BREAD

3 eggs
1½ C. sugar
1 C. oil
2 C. zucchini, shredded
2 C. flour
1 tsp. salt
¼ tsp. baking powder

1½ tsp. baking soda
1 T. cinnamon
½ tsp. cloves
2 tsp. vanilla·
1 C. chopped nuts
One 12-cup bundt pan

Beat eggs and sugar together. Add oil and zucchini, blend. Stir in remaining ingredients. Pour into pan and microwave on high for 9 to 11 minutes. Rest 10 minutes. Invert onto serving platter.

STRAWBERRY JELLY

3-10 oz. pkgs. frozen
  strawberries
2 T. lemon juice

3 T. powdered fruit pectin
3 C. sugar

Place strawberry in 8- to 12-cup measure with handle. Microwave at 30% for 4 to 6 minutes, breaking up after 3 minutes. Add pectin and lemon juice. Cover and microwave on high 8 to 10 minutes, stirring 1 time. Stir in sugar, cover. Microwave on high 8 to 10 minutes, stirring 2 times. Microwave on high 1 minute. Rest, skim off foam. Pour into jars. Refrigerate after cool.

APPLE JELLY

3 T. sugar
3 T. powdered pectin

2½ C. apple juice,
  unsweetened
3 C. sugar

Place sugar and pectin in 8- to 12-cup measure. Stir in apple juice. Cover with plastic wrap. Microwave on high for 7 to 8 minutes, stirring 1 time. Add sugar, stir well. Microwave on high 8 to 9 minutes, stirring 1 time. Rest 3 minutes. Skim off foam. Pour into sterilized jars.

Illinois State Fair - Blue Ribbon.

GRAPE JELLY

1-6 oz. frozen grape juice
  concentrate
1-1¾ oz. pkg. powdered
  fruit pectin

2 C. hot water
3¾ C. sugar

Combine in a 8- to 12-cup measure, with a handle, thawed juice and pectin. Stir in water, blend well. Cover and microwave on high for 7 to 8 minutes, stirring 1 time. Blend in sugar. Cover and microwave on high 6 to 8 minutes, stirring 1 time. After jelly is boiling, stir again and microwave on high 1 minute. Skim off foam. This gets very hot, you must be careful, especially when removing cover. Pour into sterilized jars. A great Christmas gift.

APPETIZERS & SOUPS

STUFFED MUSHROOMS

12 large mushrooms, stems
  removed and reserved
1 T. unsalted butter
¼ C. onion, chopped fine
2 T. green onion, diced fine
½ clove garlic, smashed

¼ C. pepperoni, chopped
  tiny pieces
¼ C. bread crumbs
1½ T. Parmesan cheese
2 tsp. parsley
¼ tsp. oregano

Wash mushrooms. Pat dry. Combine chopped mushroom stems, butter, onion, green pepper and garlic. Microwave on high for 1½ to 2½ minutes. Add remaining ingredients and mix well. Fill mushroom caps and arrange in the donut shape on a glass plate. Microwave on medium (50%) for 4 minutes.

SHRIMP DIP

1 can shrimp soup
2 C. Swiss cheese, shredded

3 T. sherry
½ C. cooked shrimp, diced
in tiny pieces

Combine all ingredients. Microwave on high 2 to 3 minutes, stirring twice.

CHEESE PUFFS

1 C. Cheddar cheese
¼ C. onions, minced

½ C. mayonnaise
Melba toast rounds

Mix cheese, onions and mayonnaise. Spread on toast. Arrange in donut shape and microwave at 50% for 1½ to 2 minutes. Do 12 at a time.

RUMAKI

Bacon, cut in half   *Water chestnuts, cut in half*

Wrap bacon around water chestnuts. Place in dish or put them in a plastic bag. Pour marinade over bacon and marinate several hours, overnight is good, too.

MARINADE:
¼ C. soy sauce   *½ tsp. garlic powder*
½ tsp. ginger

To cook, drain marinade. Arrange bacon in the donut shape on a bacon rack or pie dish. Cover with paper towel. Microwave on high 1 to 1½ minutes per slice of bacon, remember 2 ramaki is 1 slice of bacon.

COCKTAIL MEATBALLS

2 lbs. ground beef
1 egg, beaten
1 pkg. dry onion soup mix
¼ C. ketchup
½ C. bread crumbs
1 can crushed pineapple,
  drain, reserve juice

SAUCE:
¼ C. pineapple juice
½ C. ketchup
¼ C. brown sugar

Combine meatball ingredients together and form into small cocktail-size balls. Arrange ½ the meatballs in the donut shape in a glass pie dish. Microwave on high 6 to 9 minutes, drain. Repeat with remaining meatballs. Place all the meatballs in a casserole. Pour sauce over and microwave on high 3 to 5 minutes. Rest 5 minutes. These are dynamite, keep them in your freezer for company.

PARTY CHICKEN WINGS

12 chicken wings, tips removed, cut at joints

MARINADE:
3 T. catsup   *½ C. water*
¾ C. soy sauce   *2 T. cornstarch*
¼ tsp. ginger

Combine catsup, soy sauce and ginger. (This works well in a Ziploc bag.) Add chicken wings and refrigerate overnight. Drain wings, reserve marinade. Combine water, cornstarch and marinade. Microwave on high for 1 minute, stir. Microwave on high 1 minute or until thickened. Place wings in donut shape on glass plate. Pour sauce over wings, cover with wax paper and microwave on high 4 to 5 minutes. Check, stir. Microwave on high 4 minutes. Rest 1 minute.

CRAB DELIGHTS

½ lb. fresh cooked
  crab meat, chopped
3 T. green onion, chopped
3 T. celery, diced fine

½ C. mayonnaise
2 T. sour cream

24 bite-size cream puff
  shells

Make cream puffs in conventional oven. Slice tops off, reserve tops. Combine crab mixture and fill cream puffs. Place lids on top of crab filling. Place 12 puffs in donut shape on glass plate. Microwave on high 2 minutes.

PINEAPPLE COCKTAIL FRANKS

48 cocktail franks
1 can drained pineapple
  chunks, slice each in half
½ C. chili sauce
½ C. currant jelly

2 T. lemon juice
1 tsp. dry mustard
3 tsp. cornstarch, blended
  with 3 tsp. water

In 2-quart casserole, combine and mix well all ingredients except franks and pineapple. Add franks and pineapple. Microwave on high for 6 to 8 minutes. Stir 2 times. Rest 5 minutes.

CREAM BASE FOR VEGETABLE SOUP

3 C. chicken broth
  (homemade is ideal)
1 C. onions, chopped
¼ C. unsalted butter, melted

¼ C. flour
2 C. milk or for a richer soup,
  use half and half or
  whipping cream
Vegetables according to list
below

Microwave on high the broth and onions for 4 to 6 minutes. Place ½ the cooked vegetables and spices and ½ the broth in the food processor. Blend until smooth. Repeat, set aside. In a 3-quart casserole, microwave on high the butter for 40 seconds. Blend in flour. Stir in milk (or cream), blending well. Microwave on high for 1½ minutes. Stir. Microwave on high 1½ minutes or until thickened. Stir in vegetable mixture; blend well. Microwave at 50% for 8 to 10 minutes, stirring 2 times. Garnish with parsley or chives.

SOUP - CREAM OF:

BROCCOLI: Fresh, 4 cups, microwave on high for 10 to 12 minutes. Frozen, 2 packages, microwave on high for 9 to 11 minutes. Spice, 1 teaspoon thyme, dash of white pepper.

CAULIFLOWER: Fresh flowerets, 4 cups, microwave on high for 12 to 14 minutes. Frozen, 2 packages, microwave on high for 10 to 12 minutes. Spice, ½ to 1 teaspoon curry.

MUSHROOMS: Fresh, ½ pound, microwave on high 2 to 3 minutes. Spice, ¼ teaspoon nutmeg.

MINESTRONE

2 C. leftover roast beef,
diced
2 T. unsalted butter
2 cloves garlic, minced
1 C. onion, chopped
1 C. celery, sliced
1 C. carrots, chopped

2 C. cabbage, shredded
1-16 oz. whole tomatoes,
broken up
1 box frozen spinach,
defrosted and drained
1 C. cooked elbow macaroni
5 to 6 C. beef broth

Place butter and garlic in a custard cup. Microwave on high for 30 to 40 seconds. Place butter, onion, celery, carrots and 4 cups broth in a 5-quart casserole. Cover with plastic wrap and microwave on high for 8 to 11 minutes. Add beef, tomatoes, cabbage, spinach and remaining broth. Cover with plastic wrap. Microwave on medium (50%) for 10 to 14 minutes, stirring 1 time. Stir in noodles. Microwave on high 4 minutes.

CHILI

1½ lbs. ground beef
1 C. onions, chopped
1 C. green pepper, chopped
1-1 lb. can tomato sauce
1-1 lb. can whole tomatoes

1-1 lb. can kidney beans
4 T. chili powder
1 tsp. dry mustard
1-6 oz. can tomato paste

Saute onions, green pepper and beef on high for 6 to 8 minutes. Stir 2 times. Drain well, place in 4-quart casserole. Add tomato sauce, whole tomatoes, beans, tomato paste, chili powder and mustard. Stir together. Cover and microwave on high for 10 to 13 minutes. Rest 10 minutes.

STEW

2 lb. round steak, cut in cubes
1 pkg. dry onion soup mix
1 can tomato soup
½ C. water

2 medium potatoes, medium sliced
3 carrots, cut in ¼'s
3 celery stalks, cut uniformly
2 onions, cut in ¼'s

Combine soups and water in 3-quart casserole. Blend well. Stir in meat, cover with plastic wrap, vent cover. Microwave at 40% power for 75 minutes. Stir 2 times. Add vegetables. Cover. Microwave on high for 15 to 20 minutes, until vegetables are cooked to your liking. Rest 10 minutes.

MAINDISHES

CHICKEN PIECES

"Microwaves" are attracted to foods with a high sugar or fat content. So I strongly recommend you remove the skin from the chicken pieces. This process takes a little extra time, but it is well worth it for a better quality end result, not to mention the calories you'll save!

Arrange chicken pieces in a microwave baking dish with meatiest pieces along the outer side. Put your favorite topping over pieces and cover with wax paper. Microwave on high 1 piece, 2 to 4 minutes; 2 pieces, 4 to 6 minutes; 3 pieces, 5 to 7 minutes; 4 pieces, 7 to 10 minutes; 5 pieces, 8 to 12 minutes; 6 pieces, 8 to 14 minutes; 1 cut-up (2½ to 3 pound), 18 to 22 minutes.

TOPPING IDEAS: Bread crumbs, crushed potato chips, barbeque sauce, pizza sauce, equal amount of unsalted butter and Kitchen Bouquet, paprika or Italian dressing.

CHEEZY CHICKEN CASSEROLE

6 slices bread, crusts
  removed
½ C. mushrooms
2 C. cooked chicken, cubed
1 can water chestnuts,
  sliced

1½ C. Cheddar cheese,
  sharp
1-10½ oz. can cream of
  chicken soup
2 eggs
1 C. half and half
½ to ¾ C. bread crumbs

Butter a 2-quart glass casserole. Place 3 slices of bread in dish. Arrange ½ of the chicken, mushrooms and water chestnuts over bread. Add ½ the cheese. Beat eggs well, add cream and blend well. Pour ½ egg mixture over chicken. Repeat. Spread soup over dish. Refrigerate overnight. Sprinkle top with bread crumbs. Microwave on high 2 minutes. Microwave at 70% for 15 to 18 minutes. Rest 5 minutes.

QUICK CHICKEN BAKE

2 C. cooked chicken, cubed
1 can cream of chicken soup
1 C. sour cream
½ C. celery, diced

½ C. onion, chopped
½ C. water chestnuts, sliced
 thin
1 C. cooked rice
Bread crumbs

Mix together and place in a buttered 2-quart casserole. Sprinkle bread crumbs on top. Microwave on high for 6 to 8 minutes. Rest 5 minutes. Serves 6.

If you prefer cream of mushroom soup or Cheddar cheese soup, go for it, don't be afraid to experiment.

PEACHY CURRIED CHICKEN

2 cans cream of chicken
  soup
½ C. sour cream
½ C. mayonnaise
1 tsp. curry
3 C. cooked chicken, cubed

1 pkg. broccoli pieces
1 large can peach halves
¼ C. slivered almonds
½ C. bread crumbs
2 T. melted, unsalted
  butter

Microwave on high for 6 minutes the broccoli, set aside. Blend soup, sour cream, mayonnaise and curry. Add chicken and broccoli. Stir to blend. Place in 2-quart buttered casserole. Sprinkle bread crumbs. Place peach halves on top. Sprinkle with almonds. Pour melted butter over top. Microwave on high 8 to 10 minutes. Rest 10 minutes. Serves 6.

SOUPY CHICKEN

4 chicken breasts, skinned,
  boned and cut in large
  chunks
1 C. sour cream
½ C. sherry

1 can cream of mushroom
  or chicken soup
1 C. mushrooms, sliced
¼ C. almond slivers
2 T. unsalted butter
½ C. bread crumbs

Place butter, mushrooms and almonds in microwave dish. Microwave on high 1 minute. Combine soup, sour cream and sherry. Microwave on high for 1 minute. Add mushrooms and chicken to sour cream mixture. Place in 3-quart casserole. Sprinkle with bread crumbs. Cover with wax paper. Microwave on high 12 to 13 minutes. Rest 10 minutes.

CHICKEN 'N BROCCOLI BAKE

4 whole chicken breasts,
  skinned and boned
2 pkgs. broccoli, chopped
½ to ¾ C. toasted slivered
  almonds
¼ C. unsalted butter

2 T. flour
2 C. milk
2 egg yolks, well beaten
1 T. lemon juice
½ to ¾ C. Cheddar cheese,
  shredded

Place chicken pieces in microwave dish, cover with wax paper. Microwave on high for 10 to 12 minutes, rearranging 1 time. Poke holes in broccoli boxes, place on paper towels. Microwave on high 9 to 11 minutes, drain. Place broccoli in buttered casserole. Place almonds over broccoli, then cut-up chicken pieces. In 1-quart measure, microwave on high for 30 seconds the butter. Stir in flour. Gradually blend in milk and microwave on high 1 for 1½ minutes or until thickened. Add some hot mixture to yolks and lemon juice. Stir back into sauce. Blend well. Pour over broccoli and chicken. Sprinkle with cheese. Cover with wax paper. Microwave at 70% for 8 to 10 minutes.

CHICKEN HAWAIIAN

1-2½ to 3½ lb. chicken,
   cut up, skin removed
1 pkg. dry onion soup mix
1-8 oz. pineapple chunks,
   drained, reserve juice

1½ C. chicken broth
3 T. flour
¼ C. water

Place chicken pieces in 12x8" casserole. Combine reserved juice, broth, soup mix and pineapple. Pour over chicken, cover with wax paper and microwave on high for 18 to 22 minutes. Rearrange pieces after 9 minutes. Remove chicken to serving platter. Combine flour and water, stir to make a smooth paste. Slowly blend into broth. Microwave on high 1 minute, stir, repeat until thickened. Pour over chicken. Serve with rice.

WILD CHICKEN

2 C. cooked chicken, cubed
½ C. celery, diced
1 can cream of chicken soup
2 hard-boiled eggs, sliced

2 C. cooked long grain and
 wild rice
2 tsp. lemon juice
1½ to 2 C. crushed potato
 chips
½ C. unsalted butter, melted

Combine chicken, celery, soup, eggs, rice and lemon juice. Place in a buttered 12x8" casserole. Sprinkle with almonds and chips. Pour melted butter over all. Cover with wax paper. Microwave on high for 6 to 8 minutes. Rest 5 minutes.

PIZZA CHICKEN

3 chicken breasts, split,
 boned and skinned
2 C. pizza sauce

1 C. mushrooms, sliced
2 C. mozzarella cheese,
 shredded
¼ to ½ C. Parmesan cheese

Arrange chicken, meatiest sections to the outer edge of a 12x8" casserole. Place mushrooms over chicken. Pour sauce over mushrooms. Cover with wax paper. Microwave on high 18 to 22 minutes. Rearranging at ½ time if necessary. Sprinkle cheese over sauce. Microwave on high 2 to 3 minutes. Rest 5 minutes.

CHICKEN WITH STUFFING

3 chicken breasts, split,
  and skinned
3 C. seasoned bread
  stuffing, dry (cubed)
½ C. onions, chopped

¼ C. celery, diced
1½ C. chicken broth
¼ C. dry white wine
½ C. unsalted butter, melted
Bread crumbs

Gently mix together stuffing, onion, celery, broth and wine. Place in a buttered 12x8" casserole. Dip chicken in melted butter, then coat top of chicken in bread crumbs. Place over dressing, meatiest sections to the outer edge. Cover with wax paper. Microwave on high 18 to 22 minutes. Rearranging at ½ time if necessary. Rest 5 to 10 minutes.

HOT CHEESE 'N CHICKEN DELIGHT

4 C. cooked chicken, cubed
¾ C. slivered almonds
1 can water chestnuts,
  sliced
½ C. celery, diced
¼ C. green peppers, diced

1 C. sharp Cheddar cheese,
  shredded
½ C. sour cream
½ C. mayonnaise
1 C. onion rings

Combine all ingredients, except onion rings in 3-quart casserole. Sprinkle with onion rings. Cover with wax paper. Microwave on high for 6 to 8 minutes. Rest 5 minutes.

TURKEY

1 turkey, no more than
  12 lbs.
Your favorite stuffing

Cheesecloth
2 T. Kitchen Bouquet
  combined with 2 T.
  unsalted butter

To stuff turkey, push cheesecloth into cavity. Put stuffing in the cheese-cloth and tie ends in a knot. Baste turkey with Bouquet and butter. (Option: Using a food injector, shoot breast with 2 ounces of Grand Mariner.) Place turkey in a cooking bag. Add wine. Tie the end loosely so that air can escape. Place breast-side down on microwave dish. Microwave at 50% for ½ the cooking time. Turn the turkey over, use hot pads. Microwave at 50% for remaining time (microwave 8 to 11 minutes per pound). Rest 20 minutes. Pull stuffing out, no mess. Juices make an incredible gravy!

ASPARAGUS TURKEY BAKE

1 to 1½ lbs. asparagus
  or 2 pkgs. frozen
8 turkey slices, cooked

1 C. cheese sauce
1 C. bread crumbs

Microwave asparagus. Tie with a string or a rubber band. Stand them stem down in 4-cup measure, cover with plastic wrap. Microwave on high for 6 to 7 minutes, drain OR make several slashes in boxes and microwave on high for 9 to 10 minutes. Drain. Arrange asparagus in a buttered 12x8" dish. Place turkey over asparagus. Pour sauce over turkey. Sprinkle with bread crumbs. Cover with wax paper. Microwave on high 6 to 8 minutes. Rest 5 minutes.

CORNISH HEN

2 Cornish hens, whole
(microwave 6 to 8 minutes
per pound)

2 T. Kitchen Bouquet
2 T. unsalted butter, melted

Blend Kitchen Bouquet and unsalted butter and brush on hens. Shield end of legs with foil. Place hens breast-side down on slotted bacon rack or in glass pie plate. Cover with wax paper. Microwave on high for ½ the cooking time. remove foil, turn hens over. Microwave on high second ½ of cooking time. Rest 10 minutes.

For halved hens, microwave on high 9 to 10 minutes per pound. Hens may be stuffed, the cooking time is the same.

Apricot preserves make a nice baste also.

MEAT

TENDER CUTS: Do not attempt to microwave a roast more than 6 pounds.
BEEF TENDERLOIN: Insert probe so that the top is in the middle of the roast.

Baste with equal amount of Kitchen Bouquet and melted, unsalted butter. Cover with wax paper. Use a slotted bacon rack or a 12x8" dish. Set temperature setting for 90°. Microwave at 30% until meat reaches 90°. Turn roast over, reset temperature setting: rare, 120° to 125°; medium, 130° to 140°; well, 155° to 165°. Rest 10 minutes. If you do not have a probe, estimate rare, 8 to 9 minutes per pound; medium, 9 to 10 minutes per pound; well, 10 to 12 minutes per pound.

SIRLOIN TIP ROAST

1 sirloin tip roast
3 T. Kitchen Bouquet

3 T. unsalted butter, melted
Garlic powder
¼ C. red wine

Rub roast with garlic powder. Combine Bouquet and butter, brush over meat. Place on a slotted bacon rack or oblong dish. Add wine. Cover with plastic wrap, venting on end. Microwave 13 to 18 minutes per pound or if you have a temperature probe, insert probe so that the tip of the probe is in the middle of the roast. Microwave at 30% until meat reaches 90°. Turn roast over, rest temperature to 130°. Microwave at 30%. Microwave will signal when 130° is reached. Rest 10 minutes.

STUFFED FLANK STEAK

1 flank steak, 1½ to 1¾ lb.
  (have butcher butterfly)

1 bottle Good Seasons
  "Italian" salad dressing,
  make this with olive oil
2 T. soy sauce

STUFFING:
1 C. zucchini, shredded
½ C. carrots, shredded
1 C. dry stuffing mix
½ tsp. Italian seasoning

½ C. onions, chopped
½ C. green peppers, diced
4 T. melted, unsalted butter
¼ C. dry red wine

Marinate meat in salad dressing and soy sauce, at least 6 hours or overnight. Drain meat and pat dry (reserve marinade). Pound meat on both sides (opened). Mix stuffing mixture and spread over meat. Pour melted butter over stuffing. Roll "jellyroll" fashion and tie with string in several places. Pour reserved marinade and wine over meat. Cover with wax paper. Microwave on high 5 minutes, then microwave at 70% power for 15 to 20 minutes. Baste 1 time. Rest 10 minutes.

Illinois State Fair Blue Ribbon.

BEEF BRISKET

1-4 lb. beef brisket
3 onions, sliced
1 bay leaf

4 to 5 whole cloves
1 C. water

GLAZE:
1-12 oz. bottle chili sauce
6 oz. beer

1 C. brown sugar

Combine glaze ingredients in 4-cup measure and microwave on high for 2 minutes. Stir and set aside. Place brisket, onion, bay leaf, cloves and water in a cooking bag. Tie bag so that steam may escape. Place bag on a microwave-safe platter or a slotted bacon rack. Microwave at 50% for 50 minutes. Turn beef over and microwave at 50% for 50 minutes. Remove from bag and place on a microwave baking dish. Spread glaze over beef. Microwave on high for 3 to 4 minutes. Rest 10 minutes.

CHOPPED BEEF STROGANOFF

1 lb. lean ground beef
½ C. onion, chopped fine
1 clove garlic, minced

½ lb. mushrooms, sliced
1 can cream of mushroom soup
1 C. sour cream

Place beef, onion and garlic in microwave dish. Microwave on high for 6 minutes, stirring 1 time. Drain well. Add soup and sour cream. Blend well. Fold in mushrooms, cover with wax paper and microwave on high for 6 to 8 minutes. Rest 5 minutes. Serve with noodles.

STUFFED MANICOTTI

1½ to 2 lbs. lean ground
  beef
1 onion, chopped
1 clove garlic, diced
½ tsp. dill
½ tsp. parsley
3 C. ricotta cheese
½ C. Parmesan cheese,
  grated

2 eggs, slightly beaten
1 pkg. chopped spinach
1 qt. spaghetti sauce
2 C. mozzarella cheese
1-5 oz. manicotti noodles,
  cook according to
  package directions

Microwave on high for 6 to 8 minutes the beef, onion and garlic. Stir 1 time. Drain and set aside. Microwave on high for 6 minutes. Spinach, drain well. Combine beef, spinach, dill, parsley, eggs and cheeses. Stuff shells. Spread the bottom of 12x8" casserole with 1 cup sauce. Arrange stuffed noodles in dish. Sprinkle with mozzerella cheese. Pour remaining sauce. Cover with wax paper and microwave on high for 12 to 15 minutes. Rest 10 minutes.

CHEEZY SPAGHETTI

½ lb. spaghetti, cooked
   according to package
   directions (Toss with
   2 T. unsalted butter after
   cooked.)
1½ lbs. ground chuck

1 C. onion, chopped
1½ C. cottage cheese
2 C. spaghetti sauce
½ C. shredded cheese,
   Cheddar or mozzarella
   are wonderful

Microwave on high for 7 to 9 minutes the beef and onion. Drain well. In a buttered 10" glass pie plate, form crust with spaghetti noodles. Spread cottage cheese over noodles. Spread beef over cottage cheese. Top with sauce. Cover with wax paper. Microwave on high 6 to 7 minutes. Sprinkle with shredded cheese. Microwave on high 1 minute. Rest 5 minutes. This freezes beautifully. Make up several batches for a "I worked too hard today to cook" dinner.

BEEFY ITALIAN CASSEROLE

1 lb. ground beef
1 lb. tomato sauce
½ C. Cheddar cheese,
  shredded
½ C. onions, chopped

1½ tsp. Italian seasoning
2 pkgs. chopped spinach
2 C. cottage cheese, creamy
  is ideal
1 C. Cheddar cheese,
  shredded

Microwave spinach in box on high for 8 to 9 minutes, drain. When well-drained, add cottage cheese and blend well, set aside. Microwave ground beef and onions on high 6 minutes. Stir 1 time, drain. Combine beef mixture, sauce, cheese and Italian seasoning. Butter a 10" glass pie dish. Arrange spinach mixture around outside of dish. Place meat mixture in center. Microwave on high for 8 minutes. Sprinkle with 1 cup Cheddar cheese. Rest 5 minutes.

SOUPER MEAT LOAF

2 lbs. ground chuck
1 pkg. dry onion soup mix
1 egg

½ C. ketchup
½ C. bread crumbs
4 slices American cheese

Mix all ingredients, except cheese, blend well. Divide mixture in half. Place half of meat in a ring mold. Place cheese strips over meat. Add remaining meat and seal well. Cover with wax paper. Microwave on high for 15 minutes. Rest 5 minutes or microwave at 50% for 25 to 30 minutes. Rest 5 minutes.

UPSIDE-DOWN PIZZA

1 lb. ground beef
¾ C. onions, chopped
½ C. green pepper, chopped
1 to 1½ C. pizza sauce

1 pkg. refrigerated biscuits
  (10 count)
1 C. Cheddar cheese,
  shredded
6-cup ring mold or 9" pie
  dish

Microwave beef, onions and green pepper on high 6 minutes. Stir 2 times. Drain. Place meat mixture on bottom of selected dish. Add sauce and stir. Place biscuits on top of beef. Microwave on high for 4 to 6 minutes. Rest 3 minutes. Invert on plate. Sprinkle with cheese. It will melt in about 2 to 3 minutes.

STUFFED BEEF NESTS

1 lb. lean ground beef (round or chuck)
¼ C. bread crumbs

3 T. onion, chopped fine
¼ C. ketchup
½ C. beef broth

Combine all the ingredients and form into 4 to 6 nests. Arrange donut shape on glass pie plate.

STUFFING:
3 T. unsalted butter
½ C. mushrooms, chopped fine
½ C. celery, diced
2 T. onions, chopped fine

1 T. beef broth
1 T. fresh parsley
2 T. carrots, diced fine or grated
3 T. bread crumbs

Microwave on high for 60 seconds the butter and mushrooms, celery and onion. Stir. Add remaining ingredients and blend. Mound into beef nests. Cover with wax paper and microwave on high for 15 minutes. Rest 5 minutes.

HAMBURGER STUFFED ZUCCHINI

4 zucchini, hollow out ½'s
  and dice
½ C. onion, chopped
¼ C. celery, chopped

1 lb. lean ground beef
1 C. cooked rice
1-8 oz. pizza or tomato
  sauce
1 C. mozzarella cheese

Combine garlic, onion, celery, beef and microwave on high for 6 minutes, stirring 1 time. Drain and break up beef in tiny pieces. Add rice and sauce and cut-up zucchini. Fill zucchini with beef mixture. Microwave at 70% for 6 to 8 minutes. Sprinkle with cheese. Microwave on high for 1 to 2 minutes.

STUFFED GREEN PEPPER

4 green peppers, washed,
  cut in half lengthwise
1 lb. ground, cooked ham

1 onion, chopped fine
1½ C. cooked rice
1 C. Cheddar cheese sauce

Combine ham, onion and rice. Stir in ½ cup cheese sauce. Stuff pepper. Pour remaining sauce over stuffing. Cover with wax paper. Arrange in donut shape. Microwave on high 8 to 10 minutes. Rest 5 minutes.

SLOPPY JOES

1 lb. ground beef
½ C. onion, chopped
½ C. green pepper, diced

¼ C. celery, diced
1 C. chili sauce

Microwave on high for 6 minutes the beef, onion, green pepper and celery. Stir after 3 minutes. Drain well. Add chili sauce. Stir to blend. Cover wax paper and microwave on high for 4 to 6 minutes. Stir after 3 minutes. Serves 4 to 6.

CREAM-STYLE "SLOPP" JOES"

1 lb. ground beef
¾ C. onion, chopped
½ tsp. garlic powder

½ C. green pepper, diced
¾ C. sour cream
1 can cream of mushroom
  soup

Microwave beef, onion, garlic and green pepper on high for 6 minutes, stirring 1 time. Drain well. Add sour cream and soup to beef mix. Blend well. Microwave on high for 4 to 6 minutes until hot and bubbly. Serve on hamburger buns.

PORK ROAST WITH APRICOT GLAZE

1 boneless loin roast, not
more than 5 lbs.

GLAZE:
1½ C. apricot preserves
¼ C. soy sauce

Combine glaze ingredients and set aside.
Place roast fat-side down on slotted rack or in an oblong casserole. Cover with wax paper. Microwave 14 to 15 minutes per pound at 50%. Microwave half of the cooking time. Turn roast over. Microwave for remaining time. Spread glaze over roast the last 5 minutes of cooking. Rest 10 minutes.

ORANGEY PORK CHOPS WITH YAMS

4-1" pork chops, fat removed
2-16 oz. cans yams, drained
  (reserve juice)

1-6 oz. orange juice
  concentrate
2 tsp. lemon juice
2 T. brown sugar

Arrange chops with thickest portion at outer edge and bone tails, facing the center. Put into 12x8" casserole. Combine drained juice, orange juice, lemon juice and brown sugar. Pour over chops. Cover with wax paper. Microwave at 50% for 15 minutes. Turn chops over and microwave at 50% for 15 minutes. Add sliced yams, microwave on high for 4 to 6 minutes. Rest 5 minutes.

CHEESE-STUFFED PORK CHOPS

4 -1½" pork chops with
  pockets
1 C. bread crumbs
STUFFING:
½ C. Swiss cheese,
  shredded

¾ C. apples, peeled, cored
  and chopped
¾ C. bread stuffing, cubes,
  dry
¼ C. unsalted butter, melted

Combine stuffing. Stuff chops, secure with toothpicks. Sprinkle bread crumbs. Arrange chops in oblong dish. Cover with wax paper. Microwave at 50% for 15 minutes. Turn chops over. Microwave at 50% for 15 minutes. Rest 5 minutes.

SOUPY PORK CHOPS

6 pork chops, ½", fat
  removed
1 can tomato soup
1 pkg. dry onion soup mix

1 medium onion, sliced
1 green pepper, sliced
1 C. mushrooms, sliced

Arrange chops in an oblong casserole. Mix remaining ingredients and pour over chops. Cover with wax paper. Microwave at 70% for 30 minutes. Rest 10 minutes.

HAM STEAK WITH PINEAPPLE GLAZE

1 ham steak (2 lb.)

GLAZE:
1-8 oz. can crushed
  pineapple, drained,
  reserving juice
¾ C. brown sugar

3 tsp. prepared mustard
1½ tsp. dry mustard
1½ to 2 T. reserved juice

Combine the ingredients to make a smooth paste. Place ham steak on a slotted bacon rack or oblong casserole. Cover with wax paper. Microwave at 70% for 7 minutes. Turn ham over. Spread glaze over top, cover. Microwave at 70% for 7 minutes. Rest 5 minutes.

HAM/YAM ROLL-UPS

1 T. unsalted butter
1-8 oz. can yams, drained
3 T. brown sugar
1-8 oz. can sliced pineapple,
  reserve juice

¼ C. pecans
6 T. brown sugar
6 T. pineapple juice
4 thin ham slices

Microwave butter for 15 seconds on high. Mash yams with melted butter and 3 tablespoons brown sugar. Spread mixture over ham slices, roll up. Place pineapple slices in glass dish. Add ham roll-ups. Mix pecans, brown sugar and pineapple juice. Pour over ham. Cover with wax paper. Microwave on high for 4 to 6 minutes. Rest 3 minutes.

HAM CASSEROLE

½ lb. egg noodles, cooked
2 C. ham, cubed
1 to 1½ C. Cheddar cheese, shredded
1 can cream of mushroom soup
¾ C milk
1 tsp. dry mustard
1 box peas

Pierce box of peas in several places. Microwave for 5 minutes, set aside. Combine ham, cheese, soup, milk and mustard in a 3-quart glass casserole. Add noodles and peas, stir to blend. Microwave on high for 6 to 8 minutes, stirring 1 time. Rest 5 minutes.

VEAL ROLL-UPS

4 veal cutlets (1 lb. total),
pound to tenderize
1 to 1½ C. bread stuffing

3 T. unsalted butter, melted
½ C. bread crumbs
1 C. Lipton onion gravy

Spread stuffing over cutlets, roll and secure with toothpicks. Roll cutlets in butter, then coat with bread crumbs. Arrange 10" pie plate, donut shape. Cover with plastic wrap, venting one corner. Microwave on high 13 to 15 minutes. Rest 5 minutes.

VEAL CHOPS

6 veal chops, ¾" thick
1 egg, beaten
1 C . bread crumbs

1-16 oz. can pizza sauce
1 C. mozzarella cheese
½ C. Parmesan cheese,
   grated

Dip chops in egg. Coat with bread crumbs. Place in an oblong casserole. Cover with wax paper and microwave at 50% for 10 minutes. Turn chops over. Add mozzarella cheese, then sauce, then sprinkle with Parmesan cheese. Cover with wax paper and microwave at 50% for 10 to 12 minutes. Rest 10 minutes. Serves 4 to 6.

LEG OF LAMB

4 to 5 lb. leg of lamb   2 to 3 cloves of garlic, sliced

Make slits in lamb and fill with garlic slices.

SAUCE:
1 C. dry white wine   ½ tsp. oregano
¼ C. olive oil   1 tsp. parsley
½ tsp. ginger   ½ tsp. marjoram
½ tsp. thyme

Combine and blend well. Prick lamb at 1½" intervals. Place in a cooking bag. Add sauce. Tie end loosely. Refrigerate overnight. Place on microwave baking dish. Microwave at 50% power for 35 minutes. Turn lamb over. Microwave at 50% power for 25 to 30 minutes. Internal temperature, 180° F. Remove from bag and rest 10 minutes.   71

WHOLE FISH

1 or 2 (8 to 10 oz. each)
whole trout

¼ C. unsalted butter
Whole lemon

Place fish in 12x8" dish. Cover head and tail with foil, set aside. Microwave on high for 15 seconds the lemon and microwave on high for 40 seconds the butter. Squeeze juice with butter and pour over fish. Cover dish with plastic wrap, venting one corner. Microwave on high 1 trout for 5 to 6 minutes or 2 trout for 8 to 9 minutes. Rest. Fish should flake when done.

WHOLE LOBSTER
(LARGE SHELLFISH)

1 whole live lobster,
   1 to 1½ lbs.

Wooden skewer

Put a sharp knife through the first section of lobster and the head section, this will sever the spinal cord. Place wooden skewer through the tail. Place lobster, shell-side down, in 12x8" dish. Pour ½ cup hot water in dish. Cover with plastic wrap, venting one corner. Microwave on high for 5 minutes. Turn lobster over, cover as above. Microwave on high 4 to 6 minutes. Rest 5 minutes.

LOBSTER TAILS
(LARGE SHELLFISH)

Lobster tails
Melted, unsalted butter

Lemon juice, to taste
Wooden skewers

Insert wooden skewers through tails. Arrange in a glass dish, size will depend on the number or tails, shell-side down. Cover with plastic wrap, venting one corner. Microwave on high ½ the total cooking time. Remove tails to a cutting board. Remove wooden skewers. Cut through the shell and pull shell back to expose lobster meat. Pour butter and lemon juice over meat. Return to baking dish, cover as above. Microwave on high second ½ of cooking time. Rest 5 minutes. Microwave 1-8 to 15 ounce tail for 3 to 4 minutes; 2-8 to 10 ounce tails for 5½ to 6 minutes; 4-8 to 10 ounce tails for 8 to 11 minutes.

CRAB LEGS
(LARGE SHELLFISH)

Crab legs

Arrange legs in a 12x8" baking dish. Cover with plastic wrap, venting on corner. Microwave ½ the cooking time. Turn legs over, cover as above. Microwave second half of cooking. Rest 5 minutes. Microwave 1-8 to 10 ounce leg for 3 to 4 minutes; 2-8 to 10 ounce legs for 5 to 6 minutes; 4-8 to 10 ounce legs for 9 to 11 minutes.

SCALLOPS
(SMALL SHELLFISH)

1 lb. bay or sea scallops

Arrange scallops in a glass pie dish. Cover with a damp paper towel. Microwave on high for 5 to 7 minutes.

SHRIMP
(SMALL SHELLFISH)

1 lb. peeled shrimp

Arrange shrimp in a glass pie dish in the donut shape. Cover with plastic wrap, venting one section. Microwave on high for 5 minutes.

CLAMS
(SMALL SHELLFISH)

6 clams

Arrange in a glass pie dish. Cover with plastic wrap, venting one corner. Microwave on high for 5 minutes. If clam shell does not partially open, they should NOT be used.

LINGUINE WITH CLAM SAUCE

½ lb. linguine, cooked
2-7 oz. cans clams, drain,
   reserve juice
4 T. unsalted butter

2 T. flour
1 clove garlic, minced
4 T. parsley, chopped fine

In a 4-cup measure, microwave on high the butter and garlic for 30 seconds. Stir in flour. Slowly stir in reserved clam juice and clams. Microwave on high 1 minute. Stir. Microwave on high 1 minute. Add parsley, blend. Microwave on high 1 minute. Pour over hot linguine. Serves 3 to 4.

SHRIMP AU GRATIN

1½ lb. cooked shrimp
½ lb. unsalted butter
1 C. bread crumbs

½ C. onions, chopped
1 clove garlic, minced
2 T. sherry

1 C, cheese sauce, made
  with grated Swiss cheese

1 C. bread crumbs

Place butter, onions and garlic in 4-cup measure. Microwave on high for 1½ minutes. Stir and microwave on high for 1 minute. Stir in bread crumbs, sherry and shrimp. Place in a 12x8" casserole. Pour cheese sauce over shrimp. Sprinkle with bread crumbs. Cover with wax paper and microwave on high for 6 to 8 minutes. Rest 5 minutes.

SEAFOOD RAMEKIN

2 C. cooked shrimp, bay
   scallops or pieces of
   lobster or a combination,
   bite sizes
3 T. unsalted butter
3 T. flour
½ tsp. paprika

½ tsp. dry mustard
1 C. half and half
2 tsp. lemon juice
2 tsp. parsley, chopped
1 C. bread crumbs
3 T. unsalted butter, melted
4 ramekins

In 4-cup measure, microwave 3 tablespoons butter on high for 40 seconds. Stir in flour, blend well. Add paprika and mustard. Gradually stir in half and half, blend well. Microwave on high for 1 minute, stir. Repeat until thickened. Stir in lemon juice, parsley and seafood. Divide into baking shells. Sprinkle with bread crumbs, pour melted butter over crumbs. Microwave on high for 5 to 7 minutes or until hot.

COMBO SEAFOOD NEWBURG

¼ C. unsalted butter
2 T. cornstarch
2 tsp. paprika
2 C. half and half

4 T. sherry
½ C. each cooked crab,
 shrimp and lobster
2 egg yolks, beaten

In a 3-quart casserole, place butter and microwave on high for 1 minute. Stir in cornstarch and blend well. Stir in paprika, gradually stir in half and half. Microwave on high for 1 minute. Stir and repeat. If not thick enough, microwave on high for 30 seconds. Stir in sherry. Combine a little hot mixture into the egg yolks, blend this well and pour it back into hot mixture. Blend in seafood. Microwave on high 4 to 6 minutes or until hot. Great served with rice or on top of toast.

SEAFOOD BAKE

½ lb. shrimp, cooked
½ lb. crabmeat, cooked
¼ lb. bay scallops, cooked
2 C. cooked pasta
½ C. celery, sliced

1 can cream of mushroom
 soup
1 can Cheddar cheese soup
¼ C. half and half
1 C. bread crumbs
¼ C. unsalted butter, melted

Combine all the ingredients, except bread crumbs and melted butter. Place in a 2- to 3-quart casserole. Sprinkle with bread crumbs. Pour butter over crumbs. Cover with wax paper and microwave on high for 6 to 9 minutes. Rest 5 minutes.

SEAFOOD QUICHE

1 C. whipping cream
1 C. half and half
3 eggs
1½ T. flour
½ C. green onions, sliced
½ C. cooked shrimp, diced

½ C. cooked crabmeat, diced
¼ C. cooked by scallops
1 C. Monterey Jack cheese, shredded
1-9 to 10" baked pie shell

Blend eggs in blender. Add cream, flour and half and half. Blend. Place cheese, seafood and onions in pie shell. Add egg mixture. Stir to blend well. Microwave on high for 5 minutes. Stir outside of quiche toward middle. Microwave on high for 5 minutes. Rest 5 minutes.

Illinois State Fair Blue Ribbon.

CRABMEAT TETRAZZINI

2 C. cheese sauce
¼ C. green peppers,
 chopped fine
1 small jar pimento
1 C. mushrooms, sliced
1 lb. cooked crabmeat

½ C. sherry
½ lb. spaghetti noodles,
 cooked according to
 package directions, drain
1 C. Parmesan cheese

Combine all the ingredients, except cheese, in a 3-quart casserole. Sprinkle with Parmesan cheese. Cover with wax paper and microwave on high for 6 to 8 minutes. Rest 5 minutes.

SALMON BAKE

2-1 lb. cans salmon, drained
   flaked, reserve juice
¾ C. milk
1½ C. bread crumbs

2 T. pickle relish
1 T. lemon juice
1 egg, beaten
3 T. unsalted butter, melted

Add reserved juice to milk to make 1 cup. Combine all ingredients in a ring mold or pie dish. Cover with wax paper. Microwave on high 9 to 11 minutes. Rest 5 minutes.

PUFFY SALMON

1-16 oz. can salmon, drained
  and flaked
1 C. croutons
1½ C. Cheddar cheese
4 eggs

1 C. milk
½ C. half and half
½ tsp. Worcestershire sauce
¾ tsp. dry mustard

Butter 2-quart casserole. Layer ½ croutons, salmon and cheese. Repeat. Beat eggs well, add remaining ingredients. Pour over casserole. Microwave on high for 6 to 8 minutes. Rest 5 minutes.

BAKED FISH FILLETS WITH CHEESE SAUCE

1 lb. fish fillets

Sauce:
1 can Cheddar cheese soup,   ½ C. sour cream
*   concentrate*

Combine in a 1-quart measure. Microwave on high for 1½ minutes. Stir to blend. Arrange fish (thickest side toward outer side of dish). Pour sauce over the fish. Top with ½ cup of bread crumbs. Cover with wax paper. Microwave on high for 7 to 9 minutes. Rest 5 minutes.

CREOLE OF FISH

1 lb. fish fillets
1 medium onion, sliced
  and quartered
¾ C . mushrooms, sliced

¾ C. green pepper,
  chopped
½ C. celery, diagonally
  sliced
2-8 oz. cans tomato sauce

Arrange fish in a 12x8" dish (thickest part of fish facing outside). Combine remaining ingredients and pour over fish. Cover with plastic wrap, venting one corner. Microwave on high for 8 to 10 minutes. Rest 5 minutes. Wonderful served over rice.

SOLE AND SPINACH BAKE

1 lb. fillet of sole
1 pkg. chopped spinach
1 C. sour cream
1 T. lemon juice

¼ C. green onion, chopped
 tops only
½ C. bread crumbs

Microwave spinach on high for 6 minutes, drain well. Combine sour cream, lemon juice and onions. Mix ½ of mixture into spinach, blend. Place spinach mixture in bottom of buttered 12x8" casserole. Place fish over spinach (thickest part of fish towards outside). Pour remaining sauce over fish. Sprinkle with bread crumbs. Cover with wax paper. Microwave on high for 8 to 10 minutes. Rest 5 minutes.

TUNA BURGERS

4 hamburger buns
1-7 oz. can tuna, drained
3 T. onion, chopped
3 T. celery, chopped

3 T. mayonnaise
4 slices American cheese
  (orCheddar.)

Mix tuna, onion, celery and mayonnaise, set aside. Mix 3 tablespoons mayonnaise and 3 tablespoons catsup and spread on bottom of 4 buns. Place cheese on bun, then tuna mixture. Wrap in a paper towel. Microwave on high for 2 to 3 minutes.

VEGETABLES

VEGETABLE FACTS

1. When preparing fresh vegetables, cut in uniform pieces.
2. Use salt after cooking.
3. Pierce the skins of potatoes, squash, pumpkins. This will prevent them from busting.
4. Microwave frozen vegetables in the box. Pierce several places. Remove outer paper and place on a paper plate. Microwave on high 6 to 8 minutes.
5. Place vegetables in a donut shape whenever possible.
6. Use wax paper to cover vegetables.
7. Microwave corn in the husk, 3 minutes per ear. The silk comes right off.
8. The "resting" time is important.
9. Vegetables are always better crisp!
10. You can have calorie-free vegetables with your microwave. Enjoy this benefit.

STUFFED ACORN SQUASH

2 acorn squash (uniform in
 size, about 1 lb. each)
1 can apple pie or peach
 pie filling
¼ C. onion, chopped
½ tsp. ginger

¼ C. unsalted butter, melted
 (microwave on high 45
 seconds)
2 T. water
1 C. stuffing mix, cubed
 style

Wash outside of squash. Pierce several times with a knife. Place on a paper towel. Microwave on high for 6 minutes. Turn squash, microwave on high 5 to 6 minutes, rest 10 minutes. Combine remaining ingredients. Cut squash in half and scoop out seeds. Fill cavities with stuffing. Arrange squash in the donut shape on glass platter. Cover with wax paper. Microwave on high 7 to 9 minutes.

CHEEZY BROCCOLI - NOODLE BAKE

1 lb. vermicelli, cooked
¾ C. onion, chopped
4 T. unsalted butter
2 pkgs. chopped broccoli
1-16 oz. jar processed
   cheese spread

1-10¾ oz. can cream of
   mushroom soup
1 C. milk
½ C. celery
1-6 oz. can water chestnuts,
   sliced
Bread crumbs

Microwave broccoli on high for 7 to 9 minutes, set aside. Combine cheese, soups and milk, microwave on high 4 minutes. Saute butter, onions and celery, microwave on high 1 minute. Combine cheese mixture with onions, broccoli and celery. Add water chestnuts, stir well. Butter 2 casserole dishes. Layer noodles, vegetables and repeat. Sprinkle bread crumbs on top. Microwave one dish at a time. Microwave on high 12 to 14 minutes. Rest 5 minutes. Serves 10 to 12.

GLAZED CARROTS

6 medium carrots, washed
and sliced
2 T. unsalted butter
4 T. brown sugar

1 tsp. dry mustard
2 T. orange juice
2 tsp. cornstarch

Combine carrots, butter and brown sugar in a 1- or 2-quart casserole. Cover with plastic wrap and microwave on high for 9 to 10 minutes. Stir after 5 minutes. Combine mustard, orange juice and cornstarch. Pour over carrots. Microwave on high 2 to 3 minutes or until thickened. Serves 4.

PARTY CARROTS

3¾ C. carrots, sliced medium
½ C. water
5 T. honey
½ C. apples, peeled, cored
   diced
½ C. raisins

1 T. lemon juice
1 T. unsalted butter
1 T. flour
1-8 oz. crushed pineapple,
   drained

Place carrots and water in a 2-quart dish. Cover with plastic wrap. Microwave on high 10 minutes, stirring 1 time. Stir in honey, lemon juice. Cover and microwave on high 5 minutes. Microwave butter 30 seconds. Stir in flour. Add this to carrots. Stir well. Add raisins, pineapple and apples. Microwave on high 5 minutes. Rest 5 to 10 minutes.

CREAMY HASH BROWNS

1 lb. hash browns, cubed
 style
1 can cream of chicken soup
 (for cheese flavor, use
 Cheddar cheese soup)
¾ C. sour cream

½ C. onions, chopped
¼ C. green pepper, diced
¼ C. celery, diced
3 T. unsalted butter
¾ C. Cheddar cheese
1 C. bread crumbs, for
 topping

Microwave hash browns at 50% for 5 minutes. Combine potatoes with remaining ingredients (except bread crumbs). Place in a 2-quart microwave casserole. Sprinkle with bread crumbs. Microwave on high 10 to 12 minutes. Rest 5 minutes.

POTATO AU GRATIN

4 medium potatoes
2 C. cheese sauce

¾ to 1 C. bread crumbs

slice potatoes in half. Place cut-side down in a plastic bag leaving end of bag open. Microwave on high for 10 to 12 minutes, rest 5 minutes. Peel and slice potatoes. Combine potatoes and cheese sauce in a 2-quart casserole. Sprinkle with bread crumbs. Cover with wax paper and microwave on high 4 to 6 minutes, until hot and bubbly.

SWEET POTATO/APPLE BAKE

3 medium sweet potatoes
3 apples, Granny Smith are
  excellent

¼ C. unsalted butter
¾ C. brown sugar
⅓ C. water

Slice potatoes in half lengthwise. Place inside a plastic bag, cut side down, leaving end of bag open. Microwave on high 7 to 8 minutes. Rest 5 minutes. Peel and slice. Arrange potato slices in a 2-quart baking dish. Core, peel and slice apples. Add apples to potatoes. Dot butter, brown sugar and water over casserole. Cover with wax paper. Microwave at 70% power for 10 minutes. Rest 3 minutes. Serves 4.

STUFFED TOMATOES

1 box chopped broccoli
3 medium tomatoes, cut in
  half

½ C. Swiss cheese
½ C. onion, chopped
½ C. bread crumbs

Pierce broccoli box in several places. Microwave on high 6 minutes. Rest 5 minutes. Combine broccoli, cheese, onion. Mound on top of tomatoes. Arrange in donut shape on glass plate. Sprinkle with bread crumbs, microwave on high 2 to 3 minutes.

SPINACH SALAD

Fresh spinach, washed and
  dried
5 slices bacon, more if you
  prefer
1 small onion, thin sliced

6 T. bacon drippings
6 T. sugar
6 T. vinegar
½ tsp. garlic powder
¼ tsp. dry mustard
3 hard-boiled eggs, sliced

Microwave bacon on high for 5 to 7 minutes, reserve drippings. Combine spinach and onion in serving bowl, add crumbled bacon. Combine remaining ingredients (except eggs). Microwave on high for 45 to 60 seconds. Stir. Pour over spinach and toss. Garnish with egg slices.

DILLY SPINACH PIE

2 pkgs. chopped spinach	1½ C. feta cheese
¼ C. flour, sifted with	1½ tsp. dill
½ tsp. baking powder	4 eggs
1 to 2 garlic cloves, minced	½ C. milk, combined with
	½ C. half and half

Microwave spinach in box on high for 8 to 10 minutes. Drain well. Beat eggs until thickened and lemon colored. Add garlic and cheese. Sift flour and baking powder together. Add to egg mixture alternating with milk and cream. Add well-drained spinach and blend, stir in dill. Butter a 9" casserole. Add spinach mixture. Microwave at 80% for 15 minutes. Rest 5 minutes. Serves 4 to 6.

SPINACH QUICHE

1 box chopped spinach,
   defrosted and well
   drained
1 C. half and half
1 C. whipping cream
3 eggs
1½ T. flour

1 C. Cheddar cheese
   (Monterey Jack or Swiss
   may also be a good
   choice)
½ C. onion, chopped
1 tsp. dill weed

Blend eggs in blender. Add cream, half and half and flour. Blend. Place cheese, spinach, onion and dill in 1 baked 9 or 10" pie crust. Add egg mixture. Stir well. Microwave on high 5 minutes. Stir outside of quiche towards the middle. Microwave on high for 5 minutes. Rest 5 minutes.

VEGETABLE MEDLEY

1 pkg. peas and carrots
1 pkg. cut green beans
1 can water chestnuts
  sliced
½ C. mushrooms, sauteed

1 can cream of mushroom or
  cream of celery soup
4 T. sherry
1 C. Cheddar cheese,
  shredded
½ C. bread crumbs

Poke holes in vegetable boxes and microwave on high 9 minutes, drain well. Combine all ingredients, except bread crumbs, blend well. Place in 2-quart buttered casserole. Sprinkle with bread crumbs. Microwave on high 7 to 9 minutes. Rest 5 minutes.

ZUCCHINI

1 lb. zucchini, julienned
½ C. onions, sliced

2 T. unsalted butter
4 T. Parmesan cheese

Place zucchini, onion and butter in a 1-quart casserole. Cover with wax paper. Microwave on high 5 to 7 minutes (do not cook them soft, crunchy is always better). Sprinkle with Parmesan cheese. Toss gently.

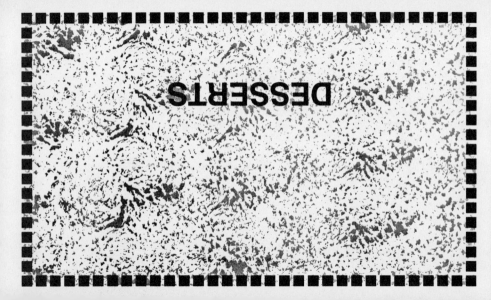

DESSERTS

MINT CHIP POUND CAKE

1-16 oz. pound cake mix   ½ C. milk
2 eggs   2 C. mint chocolate chips

Microwave ½ cup mint chips on medium, 50%, for 1 to 2 minutes. Stir until smooth. Combine melted chocolate with cake mix, eggs, and milk. Beat 4 minutes with electric mixer. Fold in 1½ cup mint chips. Pour into desired dish and microwave.

8" SQUARE PAN: Microwave at 50% for 3 minutes, then microwave on high 3 minutes. This will use about 2½ cups batter.

9" ROUND PAN: Microwave at 50% for 3 minutes, then microwave on high 3 minutes. This will use 3 cups batter.

6-CUP RING MOLD: Microwave at 50% for 3 minutes. Then microwave on high 2½ minutes. This will use 2½ cups batter. Rest 5 minutes. Remove to serving plate. Sprinkle with chocolate powdered sugar.

DELUXE CARROT CAKE

4 eggs	1¼ tsp. cloves
1½ C. sugar	¾ tsp. salt
1¼ C. oil	2¾ C. grated raw carrots
2 C. flour	¾ C. nuts, chopped
2 tsp. baking soda	1 tsp. vanilla
2½ tsp. cinnamon	One 12-cup bundt pan

Beat eggs until well blended. Add sugar and blend well. Beat in oil (¼ cup at a time). Combine flour, baking soda, cinnamon, cloves and salt in a large bowl. Add egg mixture to flour mixture and blend well. Add carrots, nuts and vanilla, mix until blended. Pour into bundt pan. Microwave on high for 14 to 15 minutes. Rest 10 minutes. Loosen sides and center. Invert on serving plate. Frost with Cream Cheese Frosting (next recipe).

CREAM CHEESE FROSTING

8 oz. cream cheese
6 T. unsalted butter

1 lb. confectioners' sugar
2 tsp. vanilla

In a 2-quart dish, microwave cream cheese and butter on high for 45 seconds. Blend well. Add sugar and vanilla until fluffy. Drizzle over cake.

MOISTEST CAKE EVER

1 (2 layer) cake mix   *2 eggs*
1 can pie filling

Mix ingredients together. Pour into desired pan.
FOR 12-CUP BUNDT: Microwave on high for 10 to 12 minutes.
FOR 6-CUP RING MOLD: Microwave on high for 6 to 7 minutes.
FOR 6 CUPCAKES: Microwave on high for 2 minutes and 45 seconds. Rest 5 minutes.
SUGGESTIONS: White cake with blueberry pie filling; devil's food cake with cherry pie filling; yellow cake with peach pie filling; spice cake with apple pie filling.

SUPER CUPCAKES

1 pkg. (2 layer) chocolate
cake mix (prepare with
¼ C. less liquid)

1 batch cream cheese recipe
Microwave muffin pan
Paper liners

Place liners in pan. Add about 2 tablespoons batter in each cup. Add about 1 tablespoon of cream cheese mix over batter. Microwave on high for 2¾ to 3 minutes. Rest 3 minutes. Sprinkle powdered sugar on top.

PUMPKIN STEAMED PUDDING CAKE

¾ C. unsalted butter
¾ C. sugar
¾ C. brown sugar
4 eggs
2½ C. flour
½ tsp. cloves
1 tsp. ginger
2 tsp. cinnamon

2 tsp. baking soda
½ tsp. salt
½ tsp. baking powder
2 C. pumpkin
1 C. milk
One 12-cup bundt pan or
two 6-cup ring molds

Blend butter and sugars well. Add eggs and beat until blended. Combine flour and spices. Combine pumpkin and milk. Alternate flour and pumpkin mixture into egg mixture. Pour into pan. For 12-cup bundt pan, microwave on medium (50%) for 15 minutes, then microwave on high for 5 minutes. Rest 5 minutes. For 6-cup (do one at a time) ring mold, microwave at 50% for 11 minutes, then microwave on high 3 to 4 minutes.

PUMPKIN CUPCAKES

1 C. sugar	½ tsp. salt
⅓ C. Crisco	1 tsp. cinnamon
2 eggs	½ tsp. cloves
1 C. pumpkin	½ tsp. nutmeg
1⅓ C. flour	½ tsp. vanilla
1 tsp. baking soda	⅓ C. water
¼ tsp. baking powder	½ to ¾ C. nuts, chopped

Beat sugar, shortening and eggs, blend well. Stir in pumpkin, blend. Add remaining dry ingredients. Mix in vanilla and water. Stir in nuts. Microwave 6 cupcakes at a time in a paper-lined muffin pan on medium (50%) for 3½ to 5 minutes.

PUMPKIN PIE

1 lb. pumpkin	2 eggs
1 C. brown sugar	1 C. half and half
1 tsp. cinnamon	½ C. whipping cream
½ tsp. ginger	1 baked pie shell
½ tsp. cloves	

Put eggs in blender, process until well beaten. Add remaining ingredients. Blend, pour into pie shell. Microwave on medium (50%) 12 to 14 minutes. Stir to rearrange liquid every 5 minutes. Continue to microwave at 50% for 6 to 8 minutes OR microwave on high for 4 to 5 minutes, stir outside toward middle. Microwave on high for 5 to 6 minutes. Rest and cool.

CHEESY APPLE PIE

6 to 7 Granny Smith apples,
  peeled, cored and
  sliced
½ to ¾ C. sugar
2½ T. flour
1½ tsp. lemon peel
2 tsp. cinnamon
½ tsp. cloves

CRUMB TOPPING:
4 T. unsalted butter, melted
½ C. flour
½ to ¾ C. Cheddar cheese,
  sharp
3 T. sugar

1 baked pie crust, for this pie I use a basic pie crust recipe, substituting 3 to 4 tablespoons sour cream in place of the ice water. Mix apples, sugar, flour and spices. Arrange in pie shell. Microwave on high for 8 to 9 minutes. Combine topping and crumble over apples. Microwave on high for 3 to 4 minutes. Rest 5 minutes.

LEMON MERINGUE PIE

¾ C. sugar
⅓ C. cornstarch
2 C. cold water
3 eggs, separated
3 T. unsalted butter

¼ C. lemon juice
2 tsp. lemon rind
½ tsp. cream of tartar
6 T. sugar
1 baked pie crust

In a 4-cup measure, combine ¾ cup sugar, cornstarch and water. Microwave on high 4 to 7 minutes. Stir 3 times until slightly thickened. Beat egg yolks well. Add about 4 tablespoons of hot mixture into egg yolks, blend. Return this to hot mixture. Microwave on high for 3 to 5 minutes, stirring 3 times. Add butter, lemon juice, rind and stir well. Pour into pie crust. Cover with meringue and place under broiler until brown.

MERINGUE: Beat egg whites and cream of tartar until stiff peaks form. Add 6 tablespoons sugar (2 tablespoons at a time). Beat well. Spread over pie.

PIE CRUST

2 C. flour
⅔ C. shortening (cold)
1 egg

¼ C. water (ice water)
1 T. vinegar

Cut shortening into flour. add egg, water and vinegar. Stir until a ball is formed. Refrigerate at least 15 minutes. Divide in half, (*microwave 1 shell at a time). Roll (do this between 2 pieces of wax paper, no mess). Place in glass pie plate. Prick shell on bottom and sides. Put a piece of wax paper over shell. Fill with rice or dry beans. Microwave on high 3 minutes. remove rice/beans and wax paper. Microwave on high for 3 minutes.

*You must always use cooked pie crusts in the microwave. You cannot make a 2-crust pie in the microwave.

APPLESAUCE

6 apples
3 T. water

2 T. sugar, if you must
1 cinnamon stick

Quarter apples, leaving skins and core. Place in a 2-quart casserole. Add water. Cover with wax paper and microwave on high for 7 to 8 minutes. Place tender apples in a food processor, skins and all. Process until smooth and mashed. Transfer to a food mill and process. Skins and seeds stay in the food mill. Sauce will drop in dish. Add sugar and blend. Place cinnamon stick in sauce. Microwave on high for 2 to 3 minutes. Cool. Remove cinnamon.

CHEESE CAKE

1 C. graham cracker,
  crushed fine
¼ C. unsalted butter
8 oz. cream cheese
⅓ C. sugar

1 egg
1½ tsp. lemon juice
TOPPING:
1 C. sour cream
2 T. sugar

Microwave butter in a 9" pie dish on high for 45 seconds. Add graham cracker crumbs and press to form crust. In a 4-cup measure cup, microwave on high for 30 to 45 seconds the cream cheese. Stir until smooth and add egg, sugar and lemon juice. Blend well. Pour into prepared crust, microwave on high for 3½ to 4½ minutes. Combine sour cream and sugar. Pour over cheesecake. Microwave on high for 2 to 3 minutes. Rest, cool and refrigerate.

VARIATIONS: Top with pie fillings. Add chocolate chips or mint chocolate chips or butterscotch chips to cream cheese mixture.

CREAM CHEESE TARTS

Cheesecake batter
Vanilla wafers

Paper cupcake liners
Microwave muffin pan

Place liners in muffin pans. Place one cookie in bottom of liner. Add about 3 tablespoons of batter over cookie. Microwave on high for 1½ to 2 minutes (do 6 at a time). Rest 3 to 5 minutes. Refrigerate. Top with your favorite pie filling or jelly.

COCONUT CHOCOLATE BALLS

½ lb. milk chocolate
¼ lb. German sweet
  chocolate

½ C. coconut, shredded
2 C. Rice Krispies

Microwave on high 2½ to 3½ minutes the milk chocolate and German sweet chocolate. Blend until smooth. Add coconut and cereal, blend well. With buttered hands, form into balls. These disappear fast.

SINFUL FUDGE

1 C. chocolate chips
1 C. butterscotch chips
½ C. unsalted butter

1 C. creamy peanut butter
2 C. miniature
 marshmallows
1 C. dry roasted peanuts

Place chocolate and butterscotch chips, butter peanut butter and butter in an oblong glass dish. Microwave on high for 2½ to 3 minutes. Blend this well. Add marshmallows and peanuts, stir. Refrigerate. When set, cut into desired pieces.

For a change, try using mint chocolate chips.

PEANUT BRITTLE

1 C. sugar
½ C. white corn syrup
1½ C. dry roasted peanuts

1 tsp. unsalted butter
1 tsp. vanilla
1 tsp. baking soda

Combine sugar and corn syrup in 8- to 12-cup measure cup with handle and microwave on high 4 minutes. Add peanuts, microwave on high for 3 to 5 minutes, stir one time. Add butter and vanilla. Microwave on high for 1 to 2 minutes. Stir in baking soda, mix until blended. Quickly spread on greased cookie sheet. Rest 30 to 40 minutes. Break into pieces.

WONDERFUL CASHEW BRITTLE

1 C. sugar
½ C. white corn syrup
1½ C. dry roasted cashews
1 tsp. unsalted butter

1 tsp. vanilla
½ to 1 C. shredded
 coconut
1 tsp. baking soda

Combine sugar and corn syrup in 8- to 12-cup measure cup with handle and microwave on high for 3 to 5 minutes. Stir one time. Add butter, vanilla and coconut. Microwave on high for 1 to 2 minutes. Stir in baking soda, mix until blended. Quickly spread on greased cookie sheet. Rest 30 to 40 minutes. Break into pieces.

PEANUTTY CEREAL TREATS

4 T. unsalted butter
½ C. peanut butter
3 C. miniature marshmallows

4 C. dry crunchy cereal
1 C. roasted peanuts

Place butter, peanut butter and marshmallows in an 8- to 12-cup measure.
Microwave on high for 2½ to 3½ minutes. Stir until smooth. Stir in cereal
and peanut. Blend well. Press in a 9" square pan. Cool.

KRISPIE SQUARES

4 T. unsalted butter   5 C. Rice Krispies
4 C. miniature marshmallows

Place butter and marshmallows in a 3-quart casserole. Microwave on high for 2½ to 3½ minutes, stirring 2 times. Stir until smooth. Stir in cereal. Press cereal in a 9x13" dish. For thicker squares, use a 9" square pan. Cool.

CARAMEL DIP

25 caramel pieces   1 T. water

Place caramels and water in a microwave dish. Microwave on high for 2 to 3 minutes. Stir until smooth. Dip with your favorite goodies.

CHOCOLATE DIPS

1 C. chocolate chips

Place chips in a microwave-safe dish. Microwave on high for 1½ to 2 minutes. Stir until smooth.
GREAT IDEAS FOR DIPPING: Apples, strawberries, oranges, bananas, pretzels, marshmallows and bite-size pieces of angel food cake.

STUFFED BANANAS

2 firm, ripe bananas
½ C. chocolate chips

½ C. miniature
marshmallows

Slice bananas lengthwise. Place them on a microwave plate, using the donut shape. Carefully top with chips and marshmallows. Microwave on high 1 to 3 minutes. Rest.

S'MORES

Graham crackers *Large marshmallows*
Milk chocolate squares

Place 1 layer graham crackers on a paper plate. Place marshmallows on top of crackers. Top with a chocolate square. Microwave on high. Remove and top with graham crackers. Microwave 1 S'more for 15 seconds, 2 to 3 S'mores for 20 seconds and 4 S'mores for 25 seconds.

UNI-Cookbook Categories

1100	Cookies	3400	Low Cholesterol
1200	Casseroles	3500	Chocoholic
1300	Meat Dishes	3700	Cajun
1400	Microwave	3800	Household Hints
1500	Cooking for "2"	6100	Chinese Recipes
1600	Slow Cooking	6400	German Recipes
1700	Low Calorie	6700	Italian Recipes
1900	Pastries & Pies	6800	Irish Recipes
2000	Charcoal Grilling	7000	Mexican Recipes
2100	Hors D'oeuvres	7100	Norwegian Recipes
2200	Beef	7200	Swedish Recipes
2300	Holiday Collections		
2400	Salads & Dressings		
2500	How to Cook Wild Game		
2600	Soups		
3100	Seafood & Fish		
3200	Poultry		
3300	My Own Recipes		

Available Titles 1/94

Titles change without notice.

G&R
Publishing Co.
507 Industrial Street
Waverly, IA 50677